Swimming Orcas

Katie Peters

GRL Consultant Diane Craig,
Certified Literacy Specialist

Lerner Publications ◆ Minneapolis

Note from a GRL Consultant
This Pull Ahead leveled book has been carefully designed for beginning readers. A team of guided reading literacy experts has reviewed and leveled the book to ensure readers pull ahead and experience success.

Lerner Publications
An imprint of Lerner Publishing Group, Inc.
241 First Avenue North
Minneapolis, MN 55401 USA

For reading levels and more information, look up this title at www.lernerbooks.com.

Main body text set in Memphis Pro 24/39
Typeface provided by Linotype.

Photo Acknowledgments
The images in this book are used with the permission of: © Alexander Baumann/Shutterstock Images, p. 3; © Stuedal/Shutterstock Images, pp. 4–5, 16 (left); © Petr Slezak/Shutterstock Images, pp. 6–7, 8–9, 16 (center); © Silver/Adobe Stock, pp. 10–11, 16 (right); © Daniel Toh/ Shutterstock Images, pp. 12–13; © Vladimir Turkenich/Shutterstock Images, pp. 14–15.

Front cover: © lego 19861111/Shutterstock Images

Library of Congress Cataloging-in-Publication Data

Names: Peters, Katie, author.
Title: Swimming orcas / Katie Peters.
Description: Minneapolis : Lerner Publications, [2025] | Series: Let's look at polar animals (pull ahead readers - nonfiction) | Includes index. | Audience: Ages 4–7 | Audience: Grades K–1 | Summary: "Orca whales swim a lot during their day, so it's normal for them to encounter many things. Leveled text and full-color photographs bring these animals to life. Pairs with the fiction title, With My Pod"—Provided by publisher.
Identifiers: LCCN 2023031864 (print) | LCCN 2023031865 (ebook) | ISBN 9798765626290 (library binding) | ISBN 9798765629345 (paperback) | ISBN 9798765634721 (epub)
Subjects: LCSH: Killer whale—Juvenile literature.
Classification: LCC QL737.C432 P464 2025 (print) | LCC QL737.C432 (ebook) | DDC 599.53/6—dc23/eng/20230713

LC record available at https://lccn.loc.gov/2023031864
LC ebook record available at https://lccn.loc.gov/2023031865

Manufactured in the United States of America
1 – CG – 7/15/24

Table of Contents

Swimming Orcas

The orca swims near the boat.

The orca swims near
the diver.

The orca swims near
the fish.

The orca swims near
the seal.

The orca swims near
the ice.

The orca swims near
the land.

Did You See It?

boat

diver

seal

Index